50

Pebble® Plus

Backyard Birds

Hummingbirds

by Lisa J. Amstutz

Consultant: André Dhondt
Morgens Professor of Ornithology
Cornell Laboratory of Ornithology

CAPSTONE PRESS
a capstone imprint

Pebble Plus is published by Capstone Press,
1710 Roe Crest Drive, North Mankato, Minnesota 56003
www.mycapstone.com

Library of Congress Cataloging-in-Publication Data
Cataloging-in-Publication data is on file with the Library of Congress.
ISBN 978-1-4914-8513-2 (library binding)
ISBN 978-1-4914-8517-0 (paperback)
ISBN 978-1-4914-8521-7 (eBook PDF)

Editorial Credits
Nikki Bruno Clapper editor; Katelin Plekkenpol and Juliette Peters, designers;
Jo Miller, media researcher; Tori Abraham, production specialist

Photo Credits
Alamy: Kevin Elsby, 7; Corbis: Digital Stock RF, 13; Newscom: Photoshot/NHPA/www.
glennbartley, 5; Shutterstock: Bildagentur Zoonar GmbH, 9, Dec Hogan, 21, Elena Elisseeva, Cover
(background), 1 (background), 2-3, 24, Feng Yu, 19, fresher, flowers (throughout), Maria Rita Meli, 15,
Sari ONeal, 11, StevenRussellSmithPhotos, Cover (inset), 1, (inset), Vilainecrevette, 17

Note to Parents and Teachers

The Backyard Birds set supports national curriculum standards for science related to
life science and ecosystems. This book describes and illustrates hummingbirds. The
images support early readers in understanding the text. The repetition of words and
phrases helps early readers learn new words. This book also introduces early readers
to subject-specific vocabulary words, which are defined in the Glossary section. Early
readers may need assistance to read some words and to use the Table of Contents,
Glossary, Read More, Internet Sites, Critical Thinking Using the Common Core, and
Index sections of the book.

Printed in the United States of America in North Mankato, Minnesota.
102015   009221CGS16

Table of Contents

All About Hummingbirds

A hummingbird zips by. Its wings move so quickly they hum. Its feathers sparkle in the sunlight.

Hummingbirds can be large or small. The largest is 8 inches (20 centimeters) long. The smallest is the size of your thumb.

bee hummingbird
(world's smallest hummingbird)

Hummingbirds flap their wings up to 200 times per second. They can fly in every direction. They can even fly backward!

A hummingbird hovers near a flower. It dips its bill inside and sips nectar. Hummingbirds eat insects and spiders too.

Where Hummingbirds Live

Hummingbirds live in North and South America. You can find them in forests, backyards, and deserts.

Hummingbirds make tiny nests on thin tree branches. They use spider silk, moss, and soft seeds.

The Life of a Hummingbird

A hummingbird female
lays two eggs. Each egg
is about the size of a pea.
She sits on the eggs
to keep them warm.

The chicks hatch in
two to three weeks. Their
mother feeds them nectar
and insects. Soon the chicks
grow up and leave the nest.

Hummingbirds often visit feeders. They like bright flower gardens too. These fancy flyers are fun to watch!

Hummingbird Range

Range

Glossary

desert—a dry area with little rain

hatch—to break out of an egg

hover—to remain in one place in the air

insect—a small animal with a hard outer shell, six legs, three body sections, and two antennae; most insects have wings

moss—a soft, clumpy plant that usually grows in swamps and wetlands

nectar—a sweet liquid found in many flowers

Read More

Borgert-Spaniol, Megan. *Hummingbirds*. Blastoff! Readers. Minneapolis, Minn.: Bellwether Media, 2014.

Otfinoski, Steven. *Hummingbirds*. Backyard Safari. New York: Cavendish Square, 2015.

Riggs, Kate. *Hummingbirds*. Amazing Animals. Mankato, Minn.: Creative Education, 2014.

Internet Sites

FactHound offers a safe, fun way to find Internet sites related to this book. All of the sites on FactHound have been researched by our staff.

Here's all you do:

Visit *www.facthound.com*

Type in this code: 9781491485132

Critical Thinking
Using the Common Core

1. What does it mean to hover? How does hovering help a hummingbird eat? (Integration of Knowledge and Ideas)

2. How small is the smallest hummingbird? (Key Ideas and Details)

3. Where in the world do hummingbirds live? (Key Ideas and Details)

Index